Koran Questions for Moorish Americans

Cursive

Handwriting Workbook

Divinely Prepared by
Noble Prophet Drew Ali

Arranged by
Sis. T. S. Najee-Ullah El

©2024 Califa Media® Publishing

Koran Questions for Moorish Americans
Cursive Handwriting Workbook

Divinely Prepared by Noble Prophet Drew Ali

Arranged by Sis. Tauheedah S. Najee-Ullah El

© 2024

Califa Media® Publishing

Lafayette, Indiana

ISBN 13: 978-1-952828-96-6

All Rights Reserved. Without Prejudice. No Part Of This Book May Be Reproduced Or Transmitted In Any Form By Any Means, Electronic, Photocopying, Mechanical, Recording, Information Storage Or Retrieval System Unless For The Liberation Of Minds And Gaining Knowledge Of Self.

A Moorish Guide Publishing Company
califamedia.com
All Rights, Remedies & Liberties Reserved

Cover Design:
Sis. Tauheedah S. Najee-Ullah El

Cover Image:
Moorish Science Temple of America
Moorish School for Children
Philadelphia, Pennsylvania 1944

Introduction

Welcome to the 101 Questions for Moorish Americans Handwriting Workbook. This book is designed to support Moorish youth and adults in developing an essential life skill: the ability to read and write in script. Script handwriting is more than just a method of communication; it is a gateway to uncovering our history. Many historical documents, including those detailing the journey and contributions of Moorish Americans, are preserved in script. To truly understand and reclaim our heritage, we must be equipped to read these texts ourselves, ferreting out truths that cannot be discovered through others.

This workbook integrates the foundational principles from the 101 Questions for Moorish Americans questionnaire to provide meaningful practice in script writing. Each letter and word you write connects you to the rich legacy of our Moorish ancestors and fosters an appreciation for the principles of diligence, discipline, and cultural pride.

While this book is created with our youth in mind—to nurture early habits of excellence and an interest in their heritage—it is also a valuable tool for adults seeking self-improvement. The Prophet Noble Drew Ali emphasized the importance of continuous growth and cultivating intelligence in all aspects of life. This workbook is a practical step in that direction.

We encourage users to practice repeatedly for mastery. Though the workbook may be written in directly, we suggest making photocopies of its pages to extend its utility for future use. A download of this book is available for **FREE** when you email proof of purchase to **info@califamedia.com**.

Let this resource inspire a deeper connection to self and nation, as you refine your skill and elevate your understanding.

With each page, may you write your way closer to embodying the ideals of our Moorish community: Love, Truth, Peace, Freedom, and Justice.

Peace and progress to you on your journey.

Cursive Writing as a Metaphysical Practice

Cursive writing holds deep metaphysical significance, often tied to the concepts of flow, connection, and alignment. Its uninterrupted strokes and fluidity symbolize unity and continuous energy, which resonates with metaphysical principles across various traditions. Here are a few ways cursive writing carries metaphysical meaning:

Energetic Flow and Harmony
Cursive writing's fluid, interconnected strokes mirror the continuous flow of energy found throughout the universe. Each line reflects the unity and oneness that ties all things together, serving as a physical representation of harmony in motion. Writing in cursive can inspire mindfulness and a deeper connection to the seamless rhythm of life.

Mind-Body-Spirit Connection
Writing in cursive engages the mind, body, and spirit in unison. The mental focus required (mind), the precise hand movements (body), and the creative expression that unfolds (spirit) combine to create a practice that aligns thought, action, and intention. This process nurtures mindfulness and self-awareness, fostering a deeper connection with oneself.

Awakening the Subconscious
The rhythmic motion of cursive activates pathways in the brain tied to memory, creativity, and intuition. These pathways also allow access to the subconscious mind, where deeper understanding and hidden knowledge reside. Writing in cursive, therefore, becomes a way to unlock insights and tap into one's inner wisdom.

Sacred Geometry and Symbolism
The loops, curves, and arcs of cursive writing resemble sacred geometric patterns, often seen as visual representations of universal truths. Each letter can function as a meditative symbol, with its form reinforcing balance, intention, and connection to the cosmic order.

Manifestation Through Intent
Cursive writing transforms the act of writing into a deliberate, rhythmic practice where thoughts and actions align. This intentionality turns written words into a tool for manifestation, where each stroke serves to reinforce focus, clarity, and purpose.

Through these elements, cursive writing becomes much more than a practical skill—it is a tool for cultivating mindfulness, alignment, and a deeper sense of connection to both oneself and the greater whole.

Helpful Tips for Handwriting Success

- Hold the Pen or Pencil Correctly: Grip the pen or pencil lightly between your thumb and index finger, allowing it to rest on your middle finger. Avoid gripping too tightly, as this can cause discomfort and fatigue.

- Maintain Proper Posture: Sit up straight with both feet flat on the floor and your back supported. Keep your writing surface at a comfortable height to prevent strain on your neck and shoulders.

- Angle Your Paper: Tilt the paper slightly to match the natural angle of your hand when writing. Right-handed individuals should tilt the top of the paper slightly to the left, and left-handed individuals should tilt it to the right.

- Use Smooth, Controlled Movements: Focus on making your strokes fluid and deliberate. Avoid rushing, as handwriting improves with consistent, careful practice.

- Take Breaks as Needed: Pause occasionally to stretch your hands, wrists, and shoulders to prevent fatigue during longer practice sessions.

- Write with Proper Pressure: Apply gentle but firm pressure on the paper. Too much pressure can tear the page, while too little may make your writing faint.

- Keep Your Workspace Tidy: A clean, organized space helps you focus and prevents distractions during practice.

- Start with Warm-Up Exercises: Before practicing letters, try drawing simple shapes like circles and lines to loosen up your hand and improve control.

These tips, combined with consistent practice, will help you develop neat, confident script handwriting that connects you to the rich traditions of our Moorish heritage.

Script Alphabet Guide

a *a* a a a
active able adept

b *b* b b b
begin beauty

c *c* c c c
create charity

d *d* d d d
divine duty

e *e* e e e
eternal elohim

f *f* f f f
freedom faith

M *M*   m   m   m

mother mercy

N *N*   n   n   n

noble national

O *O*   o   o   o

original oracle

P *P*   p   p   p

prophet peace

Q *Q*   q   q   q

quiet quest

R *R*   r   r   r

royal rise

s   s   s

sincere   seven

t   t   t

temple   truth

u   u   u

unity   universe

v   v   v

virtue   vision

w   w   w

will   wisdom

x   x   x

xenophile

Y y

year young

y y y

Z z

zero zig-zag-zig

z z z

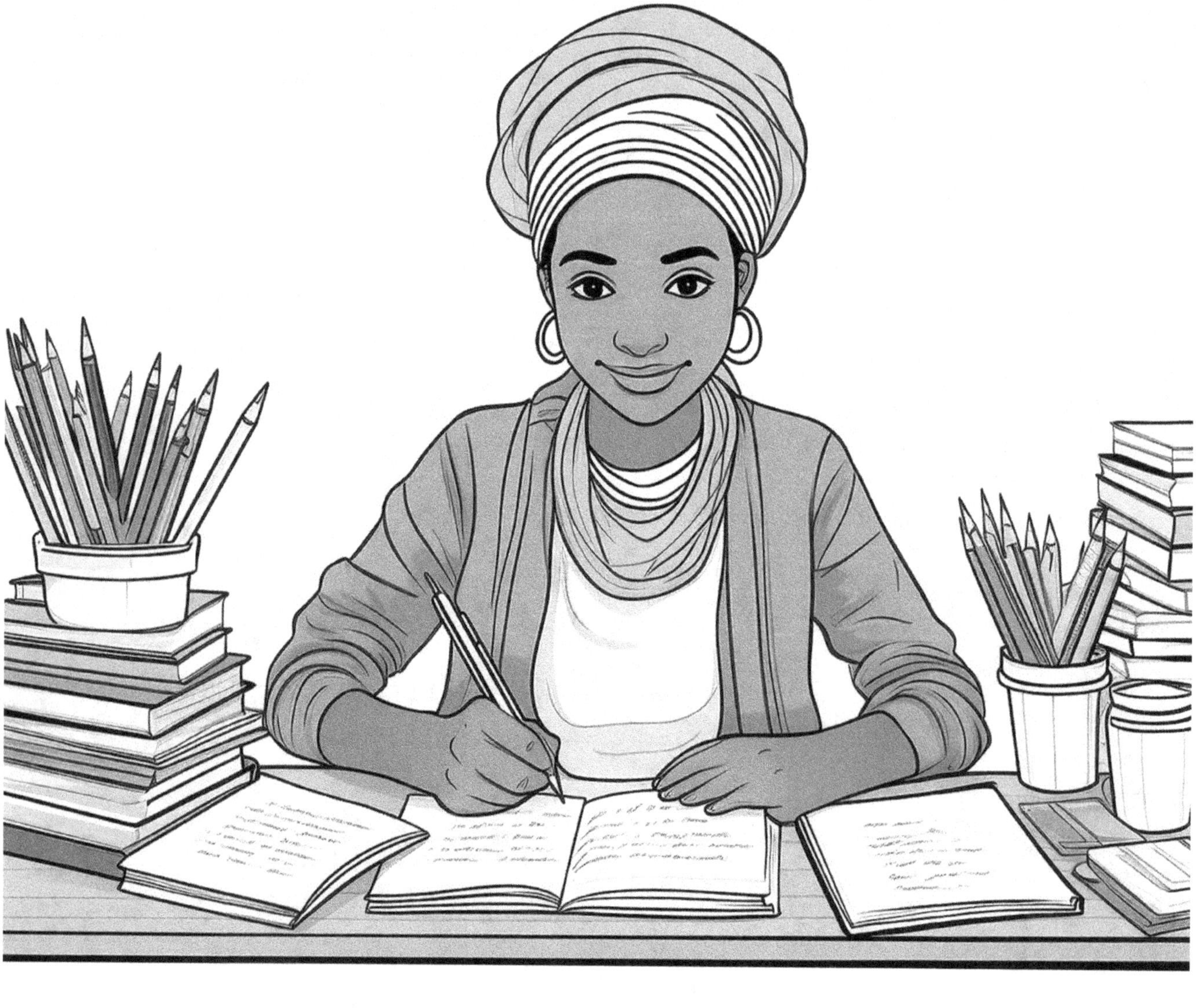

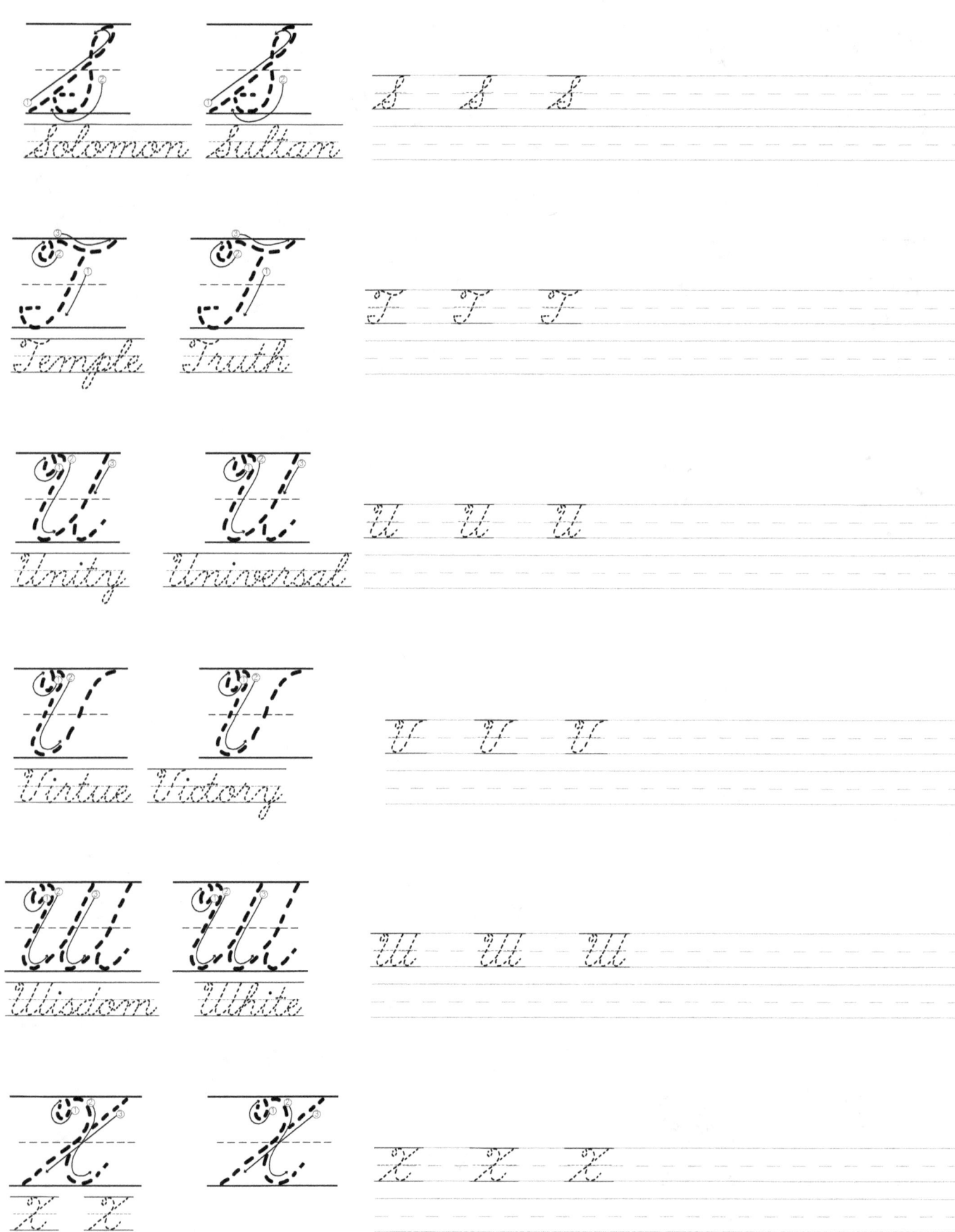

Yahweh   Yoke

Joan   Jen

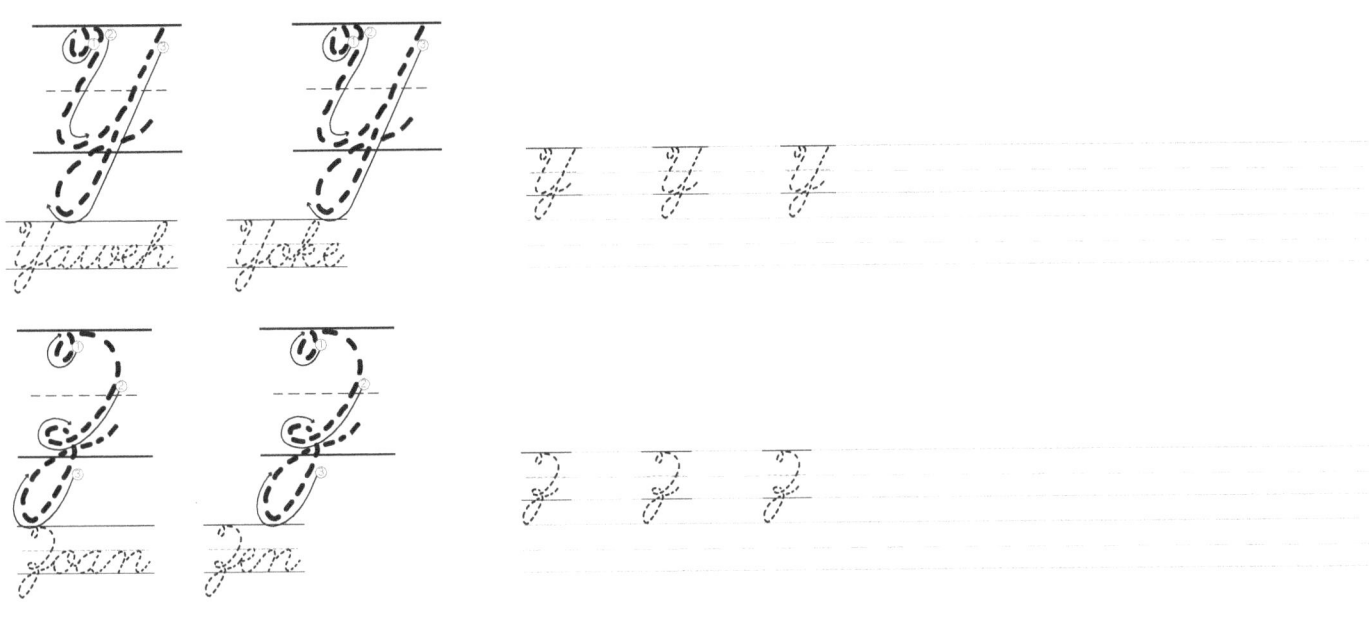

Koran Questions for Moorish Americans

1. Who made you? ALLAH.

2. Who is ALLAH? ALLAH is the father of the Universe.

3. Can we see Him? No.

4. Where is the nearest place we can meet HIM? In the heart.

5. Who is Noble Drew Ali? He is ALLAH'S Prophet.

6. What is a Prophet? A Prophet is a thought of ALLAH manifested in flesh.

7. What is the duty of a Prophet? To save nations from the wrath of ALLAH.

8. Who is the founder of the MOORISH SCIENCE TEMPLE OF AMERICA? Noble Drew Ali.

9. What year was the MOORISH SCIENCE TEMPLE OF AMERICA founded? 1913 A.D.

10. Where? Newark, N.J.

11. Where was NOBLE DREW ALI born? In the State of North Carolina.

12. What is his nationality? Moorish American.

13. What is your nationality? Moorish American.

14. Why are we Moorish Americans? Because we are descendants of Moroccans and born in America.

15. For what purpose was the Moorish Science Temple of America founded? For the uplifting of fallen humanity.

16. How did the Prophet begin to uplift the Moorish Americans? By teaching them to be themselves.

17. What is our religion? Islamism.

18. Is that a new, or is that the old time religion? Old time religion.

19. What kind of a flag is the Moorish? It is a red flag with a five pointed green star in the center.

20. What do the five points represent? Love, Truth, Peace, Freedom, and Justice.

21. How old is our flag? It is over 10,000 years old.

22. Which is our Holy Day? Friday.

23. Why? Because Friday is the day on which man was formed in flesh, and it was on Friday when He departed out of flesh.

24. Who was Jesus? He was a Prophet of ALLAH.

25. Where was he born? In Bethlehem of Judah, in the House of David.

26. Who were His Father and Mother? Joseph and Mary.

27. Will you give in brief the line (genealogy) through which Jesus came? Some of the Great Fathers through which Jesus came are Abraham, Boaz by Ruth, Jesse, King David, Solomon, Hezekiah, and Joseph by Mary.

28. Why did ALLAH send Jesus to this earth? To save the Israelites from the iron-hand oppression of the pale skin nations of Europe who were governing a portion of Palestine at that time.

29. How long has that been? About two thousand years ago.

30. What was the nationality of Ruth? Ruth was a Moabitess.

31. What is the modern name for the Moabites? Moroccans.

32. Where is the Moroccan Empire? Northwest Amexem.

33. What is the modern name for Amexem? Africa.

34. What is the title given to our ruler in Morocco? Sultan.

35. Where do we get the name Jesus? From the East.

36. What does the name Jesus mean? Jesus means Justice.

37. Did the Angel give to the Child that was called Jesus a Holy Name? Yes, but it cannot be used by those who are slaves to sin.

38. What is an Angel? An Angel is a thought of ALLAH manifested in human flesh.

39. What are Angels used for? To carry messages to the four corners of the world, to all nations.

40. What is our Prophet to us? He is an Angel of ALLAH, who is sent to bring us the Everlasting Gospel of ALLAH.

41. What is the Everlasting Gospel? It is a Saving Power that comes from ALLAH through our Ancient Fathers, by His Prophet.

42. What is the Covenant of the Great-GOD-ALLAH? Honor thy Father and thy Mother that thy days may be long upon the Earthland which the Lord thy GOD-ALLAH hath given thee.

43. At what age did Jesus begin to teach? At the age of twelve.

44. Where did He teach? India, Africa and Europe.

45. How long did He teach? Eighteen years.

46. What did Jesus say would make you free? TRUTH.

47. What is TRUTH? TRUTH is Aught.

48. What is Aught? Aught is A-L-L.

49. Can TRUTH change? TRUTH cannot change or pass away.

50. What other name do we give to TRUTH? HOLY BREATH.

51. What have you to say about the HOLY BREATH? All we can say is it is great. It is good. It was, It is, and evermore to be. Amen.

52. At what place on earth was the physical part of man formed? In the Garden of Eden.

53. Where is the Garden of Eden? In the land of Canaan, in the City of Mecca.

54. What is the modern name for the Garden of Eden? MECCA.

55. What is the name of the first Physical Man? His name cannot be used, only by Executive Rulers of the A.C. of the M.S.T. of A.

56. What are the words of A.C. of the M.S.T. of A. Adept Chamber of the Moorish Science Temple of America? (3rd Heaven).

57. Who were Adam and Eve? They are the mothers and fathers of the human family. Asiatics and Moslems.

58. Where did they go? They went into Asia.

59. What is the modern name given to their children? Asiatics.

60. Who is guarding the Holy City of MECCA today to keep the unbelievers away? Angels.

61. What is the modern name for those Angels? Asiatics.

62. What is the shade of their skin? Olive.

63. Are the Moorish-Americans any relation to those angels? Yes, we all have the same father and mother.

64. Give five names that are given to the descendants of Adam and Eve: Lucifer, Satan, Devil, Dragon and Beast.

65. What is the Devil sometimes called? The Lower-self.

66. How many selves are there? Two.

67. Name them. Higher-self and Lower-self.

68. What people represent the Higher-self? The Angels who protect the Holy City of MECCA.

69. What people represent the Lower-self? Those who were cast out of the Holy City and those who accept their teaching.

70. What is the Higher-self? The Higher-self is the Mother of the Virtues and the harmonies of life, and breeds Justice, Mercy, Love and Right.

71. Can the Higher-self pass away? No.

72. Why? Because it is ALLAH in MAN.

73. What does the Lower-self breed? Hatred, Slander, Lewdness, Murders, Theft, and everything that harms.

74. What did the Higher-self say to the Lower-self at one time when he met him? Where are you going Satan?

75. What was the answer the Lower-self gave to the Higher-self? I am going to and fro the earth seeking whom I may devour.

76. Has He finished his task of devouring? Yes.

77. When was His time declared out? When He nailed Jesus on the cross.

78. What are the last words Jesus uttered? It is finished.

79. What did He have reference to? He had reference to the end of Satan.

80. Did Jesus say that He would return to conquer Him? Yes.

81. What is the name of the person into whom Jesus was first reincarnated? Prophet MOHAMMAD the Conqueror.

82. Was Satan to be bound then? Satan was to be bound in part.

83. When was the head of Satan taken off? 1453 (Byzantine).

84. By whom? By Mohammad.

85. Name some of the marks that were put upon the Moors of Northwest, by the European nations in 1774. Negro, Black, Colored and Ethiopia.

86. What is meant by the word Negro? Negro, a name given to a river in West Africa by the Moors because it contains black water.

87. What is meant by the word Black? Black, according to science means death.

88. What does the word Colored mean? Colored means anything that has been painted, stained, varnished or dyed.

89. What does Ethiopia mean? Ethiopia means something divided.

90. Can a man be a Negro, Black, Colored or Ethiopian? No.

91. Why? Because man is made in the image and after the Likeness of God, Allah.

92. What title does Satan give himself? God.

93. Will you define the word White? White means Purity, Purity means God, and God means the Ruler of the Land.

94. To whom do we refer to at times, as being the GREAT GOD? ALLAH.

95. Is the devil made in the Image and Likeness of ALLAH? No, he is a shadow of our lower-selves and will pass away.

96. Who made the Devil? Elohim.

97. Who is Elohim? Elohim is the Seven Creative Spirits that created everything that ever was, is, and evermore to be.

98. What is Elohim sometimes called? The SEVEN EYES OF ALLAH.

99. How many days are in a Circle? Seven days.

100. How many days are in creation? Seven days.

101 According to Science, how many days are in a year? Seven days.